Girls and their Dogs

by the editors of American Girl
illustrated by Elizabeth Buttler

American Girl™

Published by Pleasant Company Publications

Questions or comments? Call 1-800-845-0005, visit **americangirl.com**, or write to Customer Service, American Girl, 8400 Fairway Place, Middleton, WI 53562-0497.

Printed in China
08 09 10 11 12 LEO 10 9 8 7 6 5

Editorial Development: Sara Hunt

Managing Editor: Barbara Stretchberry

Art Direction and Design: Chris Lorette David

Production: Mindy Rappe, Kendra Schluter, Jeannette Bailey, Judith Lary

Illustrations: Elizabeth Buttler

Contributing Editors: Kristi Thom, Michelle Watkins, Mary Richards; Contributing Art Director: Julie Mierkiewicz

Gibson's Tale: written by Katie and Alexa E., photos courtesy of the family; Kool Aid's Tale: written by Shannon Payette Seip, photography by Chip Mitchell; Lexi's Tale: written by Andrea Ptak, photography by Tom Lindfors, puppy snapshot courtesy of the family; Buffy's Tale: written by Andrea Ptak, photography by Chris Hamilton; Splash's Tale: written by Louisa Kamps, photography by Michael Weinstein; Anya's Tale: photos by Addison Geary

Recipes, pp. 36–37: photography by Thomas Heinser (girl and dog) and Mike Walker (tabletop); Doodles, p. 38: illustrated by Amanda Haley; Frames, p. 40: photography by Radlund Studios; Bandanna, p. 3 & p. 41: photography by Thomas Heinser; Pupcakes, pp. 42–43: photography by Radlund Studios, styling by Tricia Doherty; Pooch Personality quiz, pp. 46–47: photography by Mark Raycroft (Husky), Jean M. Fogle (Lab), Sharon Eide (Border Collie), Alice Su (Bichon Frise)

Trading Card Photo Credits: Basset Hound, Beagle, Bernese Mountain Dog, Chihuahua, Dachshund, Golden Retriever, German Shepherd, Siberian Husky, Labrador Retriever, Parsons Russell Terrier, Chinese Shar Pei, West Highland Terrier, Yorkshire Terrier—© AKC; American Cocker Spaniel, Old English Sheepdog, Pug, Scottish Terrier—© Tara Darling/AKC; Bichon Frise, Bulldog, Samoyed, Saint Bernard—© Kent Dannen/AKC; Boxer—© Gail Painter/AKC; Collie—© Diane Lewis/AKC; Great Dane—©Janet Madl/AKC

Some stories were previously published in *American Girl* magazine.

Library of Congress Cataloging-in-Publication Data available upon request.

Dear Dog Lover,

What's **not** to love about dogs? They're **fun, furry,** and **friendly.** They **love** you no matter what. And they **listen** to all of your deepest secrets. It's no wonder they've earned the honor of being **"girl's best friend."** Turn the pages of this book and see what makes your four-legged friends so **special.** Whether you **have** a dog, **want** a dog, or just **love** every dog you see, we bet the pages will be **dog-eared** in no time!

Your fur-ends at American Girl

Contents

Inspirational stories of girls and their dogs

Dog Fun

Treats to make and quizzes to take—and more!

Dog Tales

Read true stories about real dogs and the girls who own them—including a Seeing Eye dog-in-training, a show dog, a hurricane survivor, and more. Dig in!

Gibson's Tale

Twin sisters Katie and Alexa E. share what it's like to train a Seeing Eye dog.

The day the white van from The Seeing Eye pulled up at their house, Katie and Alexa E. were so excited. When they opened the door, they immediately fell in love with Gibson, a tiny German shepherd puppy. He was so small and his paws were so big—he was the cutest thing in the world! The girls knew they'd have to give him up eventually, but they tried not to think about that.

Gibson was eight weeks old when he arrived.

The twins raised Gibson to be a Seeing Eye dog. The Seeing Eye is an organization that breeds and trains dogs to become guides for blind people. A Seeing Eye dog gives great freedom—and companionship—to a blind person. Puppy raisers like Katie and Alexa raise the dogs until they're old enough to work.

Training Gibson was the girls' Bat Mitzvah project. "We're Jewish, and our Bat Mitzvah is a special ceremony that happens when we turn 13. To get ready for the ceremony, we do a *mitzvah*—something good for someone else," said Katie. "We thought giving up a dog that we had loved and cared for so that he could help someone else would be a true mitzvah."

The girls grew to love Gibson a lot, and sometimes it was hard to remember that he was not a pet but a working dog. Because he's a working dog, Katie and Alexa had to follow some specific rules for training him.

Almost every day, they practiced drills with Gibson. "We made him sit, rest, come, stay back, and go down." Gibson had to sit at their sides during mealtime, and he wasn't allowed to eat any "people food."

The girls couldn't give him any rope toys or play tug-of-war games with him, because they didn't want him to learn to play aggressively. He needed to know that they were in charge. What was the best part of training Gibson? "Watching him grow up to be a mature, well-behaved dog," says Alexa.

As part of his Seeing Eye dog training,

Gibson needed to get used to being in public. So Katie and Alexa took him places such as the post office, the airport, the mall, and their school. Gibson was really obedient on these trips. When he was afraid of something—like the baggage carousel at the airport or the crowds at a baseball game—they would talk to him in soothing voices and tell him it was O.K., and he would calm down.

The girls took Gibson to their 4-H meetings, too, where they spent time with other kids training Seeing Eye dogs. "We talked about the trips our group planned with the dogs, did training drills, and shared helpful tips and funny stories."

Gibson had to get used to being in noisy public places.

At first, the girls didn't realize how much work they would have to put into training Gibson. Raising him turned into a family project—everyone helped out with him in his or her own way.

Even with all their training, it was not a sure thing that Gibson would become a Seeing Eye dog. If he were to pass his formal training course at The Seeing Eye, he'd be an official Seeing Eye dog. If he didn't make the

Gibson even visited New York City as part of his training.

grade, he wouldn't, but Katie and Alexa's family could have him back to keep as a pet. "We think Gibson will pass with flying colors. He's good at adjusting to different places, he learns quickly, and he's very anxious to please."

The longer Gibson was with them, the closer they became to him. The girls always had a little voice in their heads saying, "Gibson will be leaving soon, so don't get too attached," but it was hard, because Gibson is so sweet and lovable! It was also hard to think about Gibson getting close to the blind person he'd be working with and forgetting all about Katie and Alexa, even though that's just what they had trained him to do.

When Gibson was almost 17 months old, he went back to The Seeing Eye. "Saying good-bye broke our hearts. But raising Gibson taught us that giving something you love to someone who really needs it is a true act of kindness."

As it turned out, Gibson did not pass his Seeing Eye test. Alexa (left) and Katie were disappointed for him, but happy to welcome him back into their family!

Kool-Aid's Tale

Even Hurricane Katrina couldn't keep this pup from her girls!

Sarah and Rachel C. had to leave a lot behind when they evacuated their home in Louisiana following Hurricane Katrina. But the hardest part was leaving behind their two dachshunds, Kool-Aid and Kiki.

Following the hurricane in August 2005, the girls and their family ended up fleeing to Virginia.

"It was really hard because I missed my dogs," says Rachel, age 10.

One day, their luck changed. A volunteer learned of Sarah and Rachel's story and went to retrieve Kool-Aid and Kiki.

When he got to the shelter in Louisiana, there was good news and bad news. Kool-Aid was alive and well, but Kiki had escaped and was missing.

Rachel and Sarah took in the news with mixed emotions. "When I saw Kool-Aid, I was so excited," remembers Sarah, age 9. "I went inside and got a stroller and walked her around like old times."

But life still isn't the same with Kiki missing. "I think she's trying to find her way back home," Rachel says.

"I had a dream that somebody found Kiki and the person drove all the way here to bring her to us. It seemed so real," says Sarah. "She's probably scared right now. I still have hope she's O.K."

Sarah (left) and Rachel push Kool-Aid in a stroller, as they had at home before the storm.

Lexi's Tale

Training and tenderness helped one deaf dog become part of a family.

Two-month-old Lexi

Right from the start, Chelsea R. could tell that something was different about her puppy, Lexi. The Australian shepherd just didn't respond to people the way a dog normally would. Lexi's bark was different from most dogs' barks. She didn't react to strange sounds, either. "Other dogs we'd had would run and hide when we turned the vacuum on," Chelsea remembers, "but Lexi just wanted to play with it." Concerned, Chelsea and her family took their new pet to the vet. They found out that Lexi was deaf.

When Chelsea, age 12, first met Lexi, the playful pup was nothing more than a ball of fluff. Chelsea and her family were not planning to bring a new dog into their Illinois home. But while visiting a friend's farm, they walked into a pen filled with six cuddly puppies. Lexi attached herself to Chelsea and the others. "It was like Lexi knew she was coming home with us," Chelsea says. The white puppy with a few splotches of gray had found her family!

Soon, Chelsea began to notice that Lexi was different from other dogs. "Lexi wouldn't come, even when I said her name over and over," Chelsea explains. "I thought she might not know her name." Lexi was just a puppy, still getting used to her new home. "I didn't really think anything was wrong with her," says Chelsea.

But Lexi is a smart dog—she probably would have learned her name within minutes, had she been able to hear it. The vet did several simple tests, such as clapping behind the dog's back, but Lexi never responded. Then the vet told the family that many people have deaf puppies put to sleep, because they believe that deaf dogs are too difficult to raise. "I just thought that was really sad," recalls Chelsea. Instead of giving up, Chelsea and her family decided to learn all they could about deaf dogs.

Through books and Web sites, Chelsea found out that people often use American Sign Language, or ASL, to train deaf dogs. Her family bought a book on ASL, and Chelsea began to teach Lexi some signs. Chelsea also created her own signs for a few special words.

Right away, Chelsea decided on sign-language names for everyone in the family. "Mom" and "Dad" were easy. Chelsea just used the ASL signs for those two words. As the sign for her three-year-old sister, Abbi,

Lexi responds to Chelsea's "sit" command.

who has long curly hair, Chelsea decided to tug at her own hair. For her brother, Zac, she chose the sign for the letter Z with an added wiggle back and forth. And for herself, Chelsea chose the ASL sign for "girl."

At first, Chelsea and Lexi worked together three or four times a day, for five or ten minutes at a time. Lexi was still a puppy, so her attention span was pretty short. Chelsea rewarded Lexi for getting things right with treats, praise, and the "thumbs-up"—Lexi's sign for "good girl."

Lexi caught on quickly to words such as "sit," "stay," and "no." But some skills were hard to learn. Unless Lexi is looking at you, you can't communicate with her. Chelsea admits that training Lexi can be frustrating. "Sometimes, when she doesn't want to listen to you, she'll just look to the side," says Chelsea. "I think she has figured out that if she can't see us, she can't hear us."

To call Lexi when she's not in the room, Chelsea has learned to stomp on the floor or tap the wall. Lexi comes when she feels the vibrations. Lexi now wears a vibrating collar. Chelsea just pushes a button on a remote, the collar vibrates, and Lexi knows she's supposed to come. When Lexi's attention wanders during a training session, Chelsea taps her on the head. "Then I take my pointer finger and put it by her face and then bring it up to my eye," she explains. That sign tells Lexi to pay attention!

This sign tells Lexi to pay attention!

Lexi wakes Chelsea up with a kiss!

One sign quickly became a favorite with everyone in the family. Chelsea's mom taught Lexi how to wake up Chelsea and Zac. First Mom gives the signal—she opens and closes her fists with her hands next to her eyes and signs a person's name. Then Lexi runs to the bedroom and jumps into bed with that person. "It's like having someone shake you out of bed," says Chelsea, who loves getting up with her pet. "Lexi just gets so excited to see you."

At first, Chelsea was upset when she learned that Lexi was deaf. "When my friends heard that Lexi was deaf," she remembers, "they'd say, 'Oh, that's so sad!'" But after a while, Lexi's deafness didn't make Chelsea sad at all. She knows that with training, Lexi can learn just about anything. With Lexi's story as an example, Chelsea wants to show people that disabled dogs make great pets. "It's hard for them to find homes," she explains.

Chelsea and Lexi are still learning the ins and outs of standard dog obedience. When they're done, though, Chelsea would love to train Lexi in agility. Lexi would learn to run complex obstacle courses, speeding through tubes and jumping hurdles. Australian shepherds, or Aussies, are working dogs—they're bred to herd sheep and cattle. Lexi, like other Aussies, is a very active, smart dog who needs a job to do in order to be happy. Chelsea hopes agility training is the right job for Lexi, but she knows training Lexi is the right job for her. "I used to want to be an actress," she says, "but now I want to be a deaf-dog trainer!"

Chelsea wants to be a deaf-dog trainer someday.

Try teaching these signs to your family's dog.

"Go outside"

"Whenever we went outside, we did this sign," Chelsea explains. "Soon Lexi caught on."

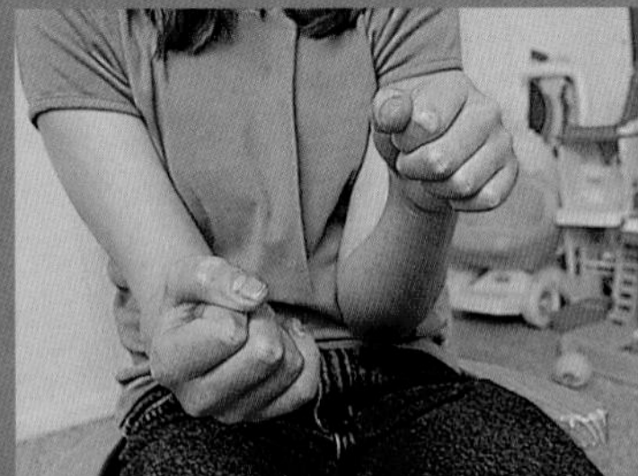

"Car"

When Lexi sees this sign, she knows she's supposed to get into the car.

"Time for bed"

Like the rest of the kids, Lexi has a bedtime!

Buffy's Tale

It's a proven fact that dogs can make people feel better. With that special gift, Buffy is happy to lend a paw.

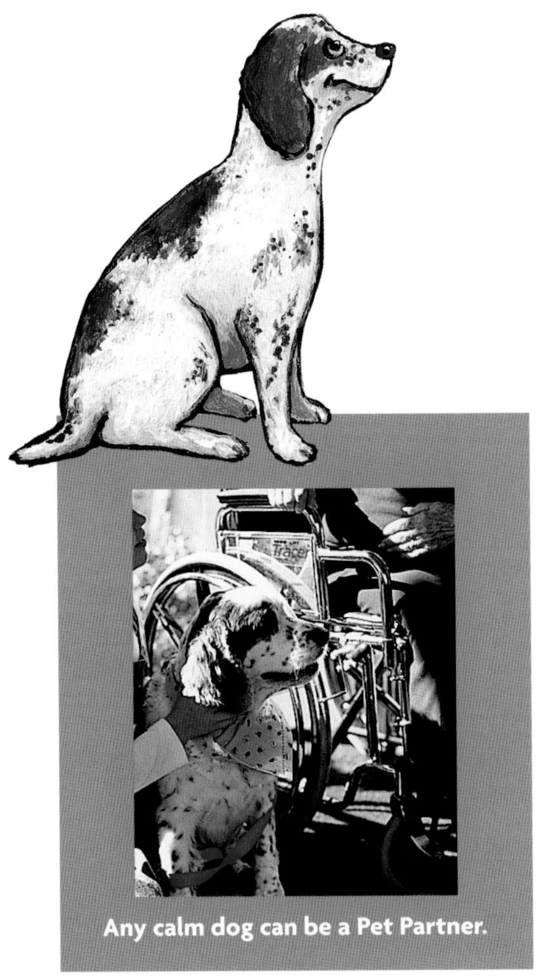

Any calm dog can be a Pet Partner.

Kristi J., age 11, and her springer spaniel Buffy, age 10, know what it means to lend a hand—or a paw. They're part of a volunteer program called Pet Partners. Pet Partners sets up visits from animal/human teams to patients in nursing homes and hospitals. Kristy first heard about the program from her grandmother. Later, when she read about how much Pet Partners teams cheer up the people they visit, she was convinced to join. Being happy helps people feel better—and Kristy knew her gregarious dog had a special talent for making people happy. Plus, Kristy says, "Buffy loves people petting her!"

To take part in the program, the Florida pair had to attend classes to review basic dog commands such as sit, stay, and down. Buffy practiced getting along with other dogs, and she learned not to eat anything

Kristy and Buffy check in.

Buffy makes friends fast.

off the floor. After seven weeks of class, Buffy took a test to make sure she would be comfortable visiting patients in hospitals. "Buffy stayed calm no matter what," Kristy says proudly. "We passed!"

Buffy and Kristy started visiting nursing homes right away. "I love listening to people's stories," Kristy says, "and seeing how they love Buffy." Mrs. Holman, one special friend they've made, always enjoys spending time with Kristy and her dog. And Buffy's quite fond of Mrs. Holman, too. She runs to Mrs. Holman whenever she sees her. Mrs. Holman, a lifelong dog lover, knows how to make Buffy happy. She bought her dog friend a special water dish so that she can have a drink during her visits.

Kristy recommends the program for anyone who loves pets—or helping people. "It's indescribable how you feel after a visit," she says. "It just makes you so happy!"

"Mrs. Holman loves getting hugs—
from me and from Buffy!"

Splash's Tale

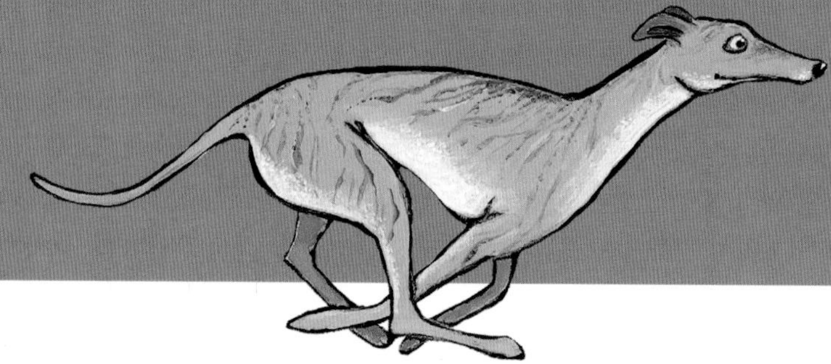

People like attention, and this young dog trainer knows it's just the same with dogs!

Tracy B., age 13, crouches next to Splash, whispering "Good boy!" into his ear and stroking his golden striped coat. The skinny dog with the arched back sits obediently at Tracy's feet. In a few minutes, they will perform in front of thousands of spectators while a very picky judge grades them on how Splash looks and how well he responds to Tracy's commands—and how skilled Tracy is at handling him.

Tracy leads Splash into the ring.

This is the Westminster Kennel Club's annual dog show. Only the best dogs and handlers in America are competing today—and Tracy hopes she and Splash will go home as champions! Tracy and Splash won many other smaller competitions in order to qualify for Westminster. But today they must perform better than they ever have before. Splash will have to do exactly what Tracy says, right down to the way he perks his ears!

Tracy became interested in handling dogs by watching her mom raise and show dogs. Tracy and Splash, an eight-year-old whippet, have been a team for three years. “Whippets are an easy breed to start out handling because they’re gentle and not too big,” Tracy explains.

Tracy came to Westminster with Peter and Andrew Green, professional handlers who have helped her learn about grooming and showing different breeds of dogs. On the first day of Westminster, they arrive at the arena at 5 A.M. Before the first event, Tracy must help exercise and groom the 34 dogs the Greens have brought to the show. Each one must look perfect for competition.

Tracy gives Splash lots of kisses when she grooms him.

Splash gets Tracy’s special attention. Moving quickly, she trims his whiskers and cleans his ears. She sprays conditioner on his coat and brushes it in with a soft-bristle mitt. Soon his fur is sleek and shiny.

Then Tracy slips on his show lead, and they’re ready to go!

Tracy’s first event is the junior handler competition, where kids ages 10 to 18 are judged on how well they move with their dogs and “present” their breeds. As they wait to enter the ring, Tracy keeps Splash calm with soothing talk. She also tries to keep herself relaxed. “If I’m nervous, my jitters can rub off on Splash,” she explains.

At last, it’s time for the event to begin. Tracy and Splash step into the ring and "gait," or trot, in a circle with 14 other dogs and handlers. Tracy is careful to stay in step with Splash and stop exactly where the judge has instructed. Next, she "sets up" Splash on a table, posing him so that the judge can examine his body shape, eyes, teeth, and coat. During this inspection, Splash doesn't move a whisker—the pair will score well in this part of the event. Then Tracy and Splash are asked to do a special running pattern. At first Splash is a little distracted and doesn't keep up with Tracy—this will lower their score. Finally, Tracy must get Splash to show his best expression. Holding out a treat perks him right up!

Splash's leash matches the color of his fur so that the judge can see his neck easily.

Tracy waits anxiously while the other dogs are examined. When the judge finally chooses the two winning handlers, Tracy and Splash aren't finalists. But there's always tomorrow!

The next morning, Tracy is up with the sun and back at the arena for another intense day at Westminster. Today she and Splash will compete in a Best of Breed event. He and other whippets will be measured against the standards that have been set for their breed. Tracy hopes Splash will be more focused on her commands today!

Once again, Tracy grooms Splash to perfection. Then they enter the ring with

30 other whippets and handlers. As Tracy and Splash trot in a circle, Splash reaches out straight with his front legs and pushes off with his hind legs, moving just as a whippet should.

Next, Tracy poses Splash and steps back to let the judge examine him. She knows his good muscle tone and the nice shape of his back will earn Splash points. *But will he be focused when it's time to gait?* Tracy wonders. The judge finishes the inspection and requests an "L trot." Tracy and Splash head across the ring and back, then stop in perfect unison. And when Tracy shows Splash a liver treat, he perks his ears with extra effort! Tracy knows Splash has done his best in this competition—but is it enough?

Tracy waits nervously with Splash while the judge makes his decision. The news isn't good: Tracy and Splash aren't the winners. Other whippets performed as well as Splash but have slightly better features than he does. Tracy doesn't mind because Splash has done his best today. Scooping him up in her arms and giving him a big kiss, she says, "You're *such* a good dog!"

Tracy also knows that there's more to showing dogs than winning ribbons. Half the fun is the friendship you have with the dog, she says. And when they go home tonight, Splash won't act like a show dog. He'll beg for treats and attention, and then he'll curl up in Tracy's bed, snuggling with her under the covers. Splash may not yet be a winner at Westminster, but he's still Tracy's top dog!

"You're *such* a good dog!" Tracy tells Splash.

Tracy's Training Tips

Dogs like challenges, so learning tricks is fun for them. Be patient and give treats to your dog only when he does the right thing. Pet him, too, and say things like "Good boy!"

Sit

Say "Sit!" in a serious voice and press down on your dog's hind end. When he's sitting, pet him and tell him he did a good job. Practice the trick over and over.

Shake

Say "Shake!" and lift your dog's paw. Reward him. Then keep doing the trick and rewarding him until he lifts his paw by himself when you tell him to.

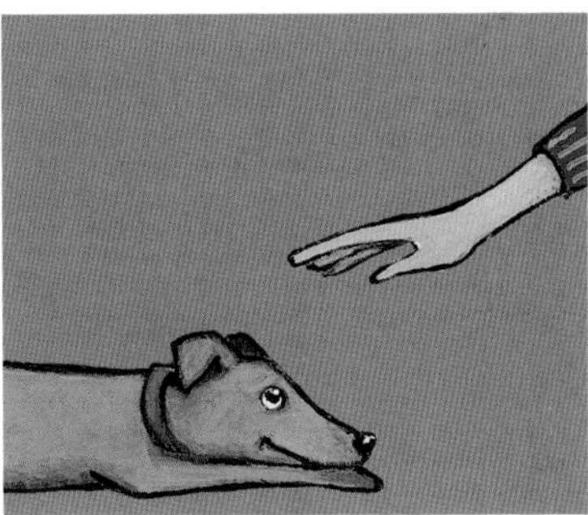

Lie Down

While your dog is sitting, say "Down!" and lower your hand so that he sees what he is supposed to do. You can also gently pull his front feet out to make him slide down.

Don't try to teach your dog more than one new trick a day. See if he remembers the trick from the day before, and practice it!

Anya's Tale

Anya, an abused Great Dane, never lived indoors until Chelsea and Shaina opened their home to the lovable dog.

Not long ago, Anya, a Great Dane, lived in a cold, lonely doghouse in her owner's backyard. When Anya's owner gave her up because she could no longer afford to feed such a large dog, Chelsea and Shaina B. and their family let Anya into their home—and their hearts.

Anya isn't the only dog to be helped by Shaina, age 13, and Chelsea, age 11. The girls' beloved pet Great Dane inspired them to start helping other dogs in need. Shaina and Chelsea's mom works with a Great Dane rescue group to find good permanent homes for the animals that stay with the family.

Unfortunately, Anya's story is not unusual. Many of the 20 or more dogs that spend time in Chelsea and Shaina's Pennsylvania home each year have been hurt by their former owners. "If a dog has been abused," explains Chelsea, "you can't even put your hand above her head to pet her, because she'll think you're going to hit her." Helping homeless Great Danes "lets you know how the world works," says Shaina. "People aren't always nice."

In spite of her past, Anya loves to be around people. The energetic dog's friendliness shows that abused animals can learn to love people instead of fearing them. Plus, Anya proves that Great Danes have big hearts to match their big size. "These dogs are sweet, really nice," says Chelsea. "They make good pillows, too," Shaina chimes in.

Chelsea (left), Anya, and Shaina

Taking care of gigantic dogs is a gigantic responsibility. But the girls know that teaching Great Danes how to behave around people can save the dogs' lives. And in the process, Shaina and Chelsea get to make friends with a lot of terrific animals. "It's hard seeing the dogs go to their new homes… and sometimes just putting up with them," says Shaina, "but it's rewarding knowing you can help!"

Dog Fun

If you like dogs, you'll love these recipes, doodles, crafts, and quizzes. Shake a leg!

Bake these terrific treats for your favorite furry friend, or hand-deliver a fresh batch to your local dog shelter.

Woof Woof Waffles

You will need:

- An adult to help you
- 4 cups whole wheat flour
- ½ cup cornmeal
- 1 egg
- 2 tablespoons vegetable oil
- 1¾ cups water

Preheat oven to 325 degrees. Wash hands. Measure all ingredients into a large bowl. Use your hands to mix dough thoroughly, adding flour if dough is too sticky. Roll out on floured surface with a rolling pin to ¼-inch thickness and cut into 8-inch squares. Place each square on a cold waffle iron (unplugged!) and press. Remove from waffle iron. Place waffles on a greased cookie sheet. Ask an adult to help you bake them for 1 hour. Let cool. Break waffles into quarters. Divide into 4 plastic zipper bags and seal. Store in refrigerator up to one week or serve within 2-3 days.

Makes four bags

Doggie Bites

You will need:

 An adult to help you

- 2 six-ounce jars beef-and-vegetable baby food
- 1 cup wheat germ
- 2 cups nonfat dry milk

Preheat oven to 350 degrees. Wash hands. Measure all ingredients into a large bowl. Mix together with a fork. Drop by small spoonfuls onto a greased cookie sheet and flatten slightly. Ask an adult to help you bake them for 12 to 15 minutes until slightly browned at the edges. Let cool. Divide into 4 plastic zipper bags and seal. Store in refrigerator up to one week.

Makes four bags

Doodle a Dog

Draw a doughnut with a piece missing.
make a half-circle.
Add ears, eyes,
and front legs.
Sit!
Good boy!

Start with a clover.
Add a circle and eyes.
Draw a nose and legs.
Ta-da! A doodled poodle.

First make a kidney bean.
Attach a smaller kidney bean
like this.
Draw a body, a nose, legs, and a tail.
See Spot?
See Spot's spot?

Grab a pencil and doodle a poodle or another one of these pen-and-pencil pooches.

Crafts

Dog lovers will adore these clever canine crafts.
Make a bunch to give as gifts or sell at a local craft fair.

Fido Frame

1. Look for mini dog biscuits at your grocery or pet store. The ones made for really small dogs work best!
2. Brush several bones with Mod Podge®. Let dry.
3. Use craft glue to attach the sealed bones onto a picture mat or frame (either onto a wood frame or directly onto the glass, as shown). Do not use a plastic frame. Let dry.
4. Insert your favorite pet photo.
5. If using a picture mat, attach a ribbon to the back with tape to hang.

Make sure you display the frame out of reach of your dog, so she doesn't try to eat it.

Beastly Bandanna

Well-dressed dogs will love these safe bandannas. Cut bandanna in half diagonally. Fold the corners of the cut edge in a few inches toward the middle of the bandanna (Figure A). Fold the cut edge down about 2 inches. Fold several more times. Make a few stitches on each side to hold all the layers together. Cut a 3-inch strip of self-stick VELCRO® brand closure and stick onto ends of bandanna (Figure B). If the bandanna gets caught on anything, the fastener will come loose and the dog won't choke.

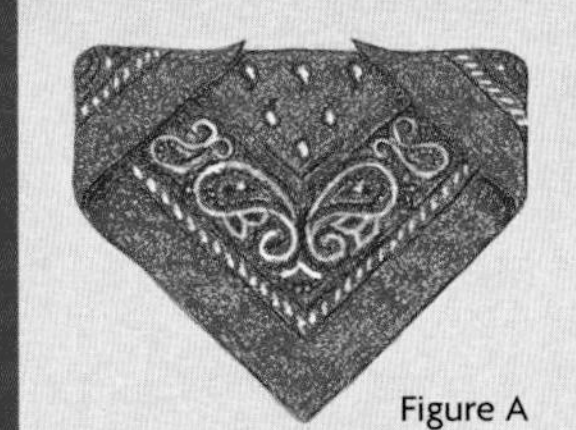

Figure A

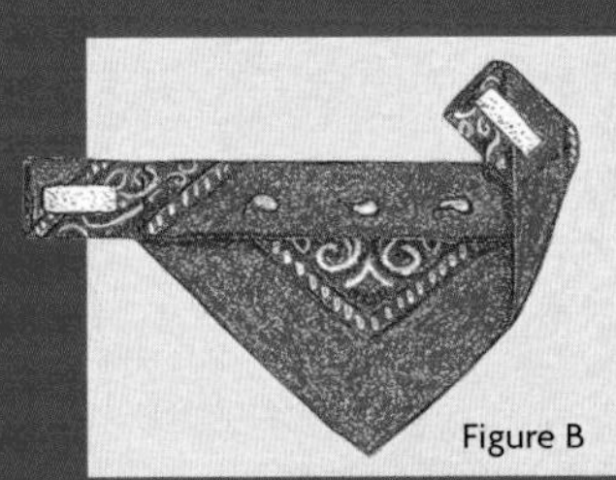

Figure B

Pupcakes

Having a dog-themed party or just want to celebrate your love of dogs? These little puppies really take the cake!

How to Make a Puppy Face:

- Cool cupcakes completely.
- If possible, try to use decorator frosting and icing colors.
- Use decorator tips and bags, or put frosting into a plastic bag and snip off a corner.
- Before decorating, practice on wax paper.
- To give frosting a smooth look, dip the frosting knife into water before spreading.
- Use your imagination! If you don't have the items listed, try other ingredients.

Ears: Cut marshmallow pieces, peanut-shaped sandwich cookies, vanilla wafers, or Swoops.

Eyes: Use M&M's, mini M&M's, Smarties (for the whites), or nonpareils.

Nose: Use a Junior Mint, Whopper, or M&M.

Muzzle: Cover half a large marshmallow with frosting, or use a mound of frosting or a vanilla wafer.

Mouth: Snip a small piece of black whip licorice, or use a dab of black icing.

Tongue: Cut bubble gum tape, a sour straw, or Fruit Roll-Ups, or use red icing.

Quiz! What's Your Pooch Personality?

If you were a dog, what kind would you be? Take this pup quiz and find out! Circle the answers that describe you best.

1. When your mom talks about you to her friends, she says you're . . .

a. athletic and adventurous.

b. fun and friendly.

c. smart and serious.

d. cute and curious.

2. When you daydream about where you'd like to live someday, you picture . . .

a. a log cabin deep in the woods.

b. a cute cottage on a lake.

c. a pretty farm with lots of animals.

d. a fancy apartment in a big city.

3. **If you were at summer camp, the activity you'd enjoy most would be . . .**

a. singing around the campfire in the moonlight.

b. jumping into the lake.

c. playing a challenging game of Capture the Flag.

d. hanging out with your camp friends in your cabin.

4. **A good summer job for you would be . . .**

a. biking all over town delivering newspapers.

b. going to the store to pick up items for an elderly neighbor.

c. being a mother's helper for a bunch of little kids.

d. setting up a manicure stand.

5. **If you could change one thing about yourself, you'd like to . . .**

a. learn how to compromise, because it's so hard for you.

b. always remember to think twice before saying something you might regret.

c. have the ability to make friends really easily.

d. be more outdoorsy and adventurous.

6. **A fun Saturday afternoon for you includes . . .**

a. running around outside playing a team sport.

b. swimming at the neighborhood pool.

c. getting caught up in a complicated craft project.

d. watching movies at home with your family.

Answers

Mostly a's

If you answered mostly **a's**, you'd be a happy husky. **Strong** and **independent**, you're not content to just hang around the house—you **love to run wild and free.**

Mostly b's

If you answered mostly **b's**, you'd be a lovable Labrador retriever. You **enjoy helping others**, but you **know how to have fun**, too! Nothing makes you happier than jumping into a cool lake on a hot day.

Mostly c's

If you answered mostly **c's,** you'd be a brainy Border collie. A **quick learner,** you love to solve problems. You're also **responsible, loyal,** and **a good leader.**

Mostly d's

If you answered mostly **d's,** you'd be a beautiful bichon frise (BEE-shone FREE-zay). **Charming** and **playful,** you have tons of friends who love your style.

12 Ways to Love Dogs

1. Birthday Wishes

Do you know when your dog's big day is? If you don't, make up a date and **celebrate!** If your dogs are all the "stuffed" variety, plan a party for the whole bunch!

2. Pen Pals

Keep in touch with friends or family members by sending them **puppy-love postcards.** Get a 4-by-6-inch photo of a cute puppy, write your message on the back, put a stamp on it, and drop it in the mail!

3. Dog-Sit

Offer your **dog-sitting services** to a neighbor or a friend who is going out of town.

4. Ode to Dogs

Write a story or a poem about your furry friend. Then read it to him! Whether he's your own yellow Lab or Grandpa's golden retriever, he'll love to hear your voice.

5. Designer Dog Leash

Make a one-of-a-kind dog leash. **Decorate a leash** with fabric-paint designs. Doodle the dog's name, dog bones, or polka dots. When the paint dries, try out the fashionable leash and take her for a walk.

6. Dine in Style

Make a **personal place mat** for your dog's dish or for yourself. On an 11-by-17-inch piece of colored paper, create a design by attaching stickers, pictures, and cutout shapes. Laminate it (you can laminate at most copy shops) and you're done. Dinnertime!

7. Water, Please!

All dogs need plenty of fresh water. On a hot summer day, put a couple of **ice cubes** in a dog's water dish. They will cool him off, and he'll like to play with them. If he's not your dog, be sure to ask his owner first!

8. Dog Tired

Sleep on a photo of your favorite pup. You will need iron-on transfer paper (available at office-supply stores). Find a picture you like and a plain pillowcase. Follow directions on the transfer-paper package. Ask an adult to iron on the image for you.

9. X-tra, X-tra

Gather up friends who have dogs and put together a **"Dog's Day" newspaper.** Write stories about the dogs, list upcoming "dog events" (such as a dog's birthday), and include pictures of the pooches!

10. Go Find It!

Every dog will love this game of hide-and-seek! Show the dog a treat. **Hide** the treat under a blanket or behind a chair, and have him **search** for it. If it's your friend's dog, ask if it's O.K. to play.

11. Jump for Joy!

Dogs love to play games. Set up an **obstacle course** for a dog in your neighborhood. Roll up towels for her to jump over and make a cardboard-box tunnel for her to crawl through. She'll have fun racing through the course.

12. Fur Real

If you have a dog, remember to groom her with a soft brush. **Decorate her brush** with paint and jewels. Remember to keep the beauty brush away from her when you're done brushing. If you don't have a dog, this makes a perfect gift for any dog owner on your list.

Dog Dictionary

Dogs make a variety of noises. Listen to the type of sound—a bark or howl—and to the pitch and depth of the sound, too.

Barking "I'm listening for every sound, and I'm going to protect you."

High, shrill bark "Something strange is going on, and it scares me."

Deep, growly bark "I'm brave and protecting my home."

Barking that won't stop "I'm bored and lonely. Somebody come play with me!"

Yelping "Ouch, ouch, ouch! Something hurts me!"

Whining "I'm upset, and I need a hug."

Squealing "Wow, am I happy!" or "I'm very pleasantly surprised."

Howling "Oh, I'm very, very lonely. I need you right away," or "I'm sick. Help me."

Howling when she hears a siren or other long, sharp noise (like a musical instrument!) "Owwww, that hurts my ears."

Sighing before she plops into bed for the night "I'm content."

Sighing after a long bout of barking "Why aren't you coming? I'm feeling fed up."

Growling "Get away."

Light growling, especially during play "I want to win!"

Snarling "I'm not happy with what you want to do. Get ready for a big fight!"

Quiz! Ears and Tails

Dogs use body language to communicate. In fact, they probably tell the most with their ears and tails. Take this quiz to see if you know how to interpret dogs' signals.

1. A wagging tail means the dog is just feeling good for no particular reason.

■ **True** ■ **False**

2. Ears flat back against his head is a dog's way of saying, "I'm scared" or "I'm mad."

■ **True** ■ **False**

3. If a dog is scratching his ears, it means he is confused and nervous.

■ **True** ■ **False**

4. A tail hanging halfway means a dog is relaxed and feeling O.K.

■ **True** ■ **False**

5. When a dog's tail is between his legs, it means he doesn't feel well.

■ **True** ■ **False**

6. A tail held high means a dog is happy.

■ **True** ■ **False**

7. A dog sticks his ears straight up when he's bored.

■ **True** ■ **False**

Answers

1. False

A wagging tail can mean he's happy, but only if it's combined with a reason for him to be happy, like seeing you. Some dogs wag their tails when they're in a defensive or challenging mood . . . so be alert and careful!

2. True

Ears flat against the head usually indicate some sort of distress or hostility. Some dogs do this while they're growling; they might bite!

3. False

A dog that is scratching his ears probably has fleas or an ear infection. If he keeps it up, tell an adult. The pup may need to see a veterinarian.

4. True

A tail hanging halfway means, "I'm O.K." The dog is relaxed and calm.

5. True

The lower the tail, the bigger the problem. If a dog's tail is between his legs, he is really scared, sick, or in trouble!

6. False

A tail held high is a threat. The dog is saying, "Back off. I'm the boss." Watch for "flagging"—when the tail waves slowly back and forth. Unlike a wagging tail that is straight out, a flagging tail that is held high is a warning to watch out.

7. False

Pointing his ears straight up is a dog's way of asking, "What's going on?" He's curious, alert, and ready for action.

Don't rely on these signals alone!
A dog communicates by using his whole body.
Even though his ears and tail send you signs, so do his fur, posture, and facial expression. Watching a dog's overall position is the key to understanding his body language.

Nose to Toes

Although there are as many variations as there are breeds, here are some interesting facts about all dogs.

Dogs are able to hear a wider range of sounds than humans, recognizing noises up to 40,000 cycles higher.

Dogs have a sense of smell that is about 12 million times more sensitive than a human's!

Dogs can find their way home from a long distance by the shortest route, without needing any landmarks recognizable to humans.

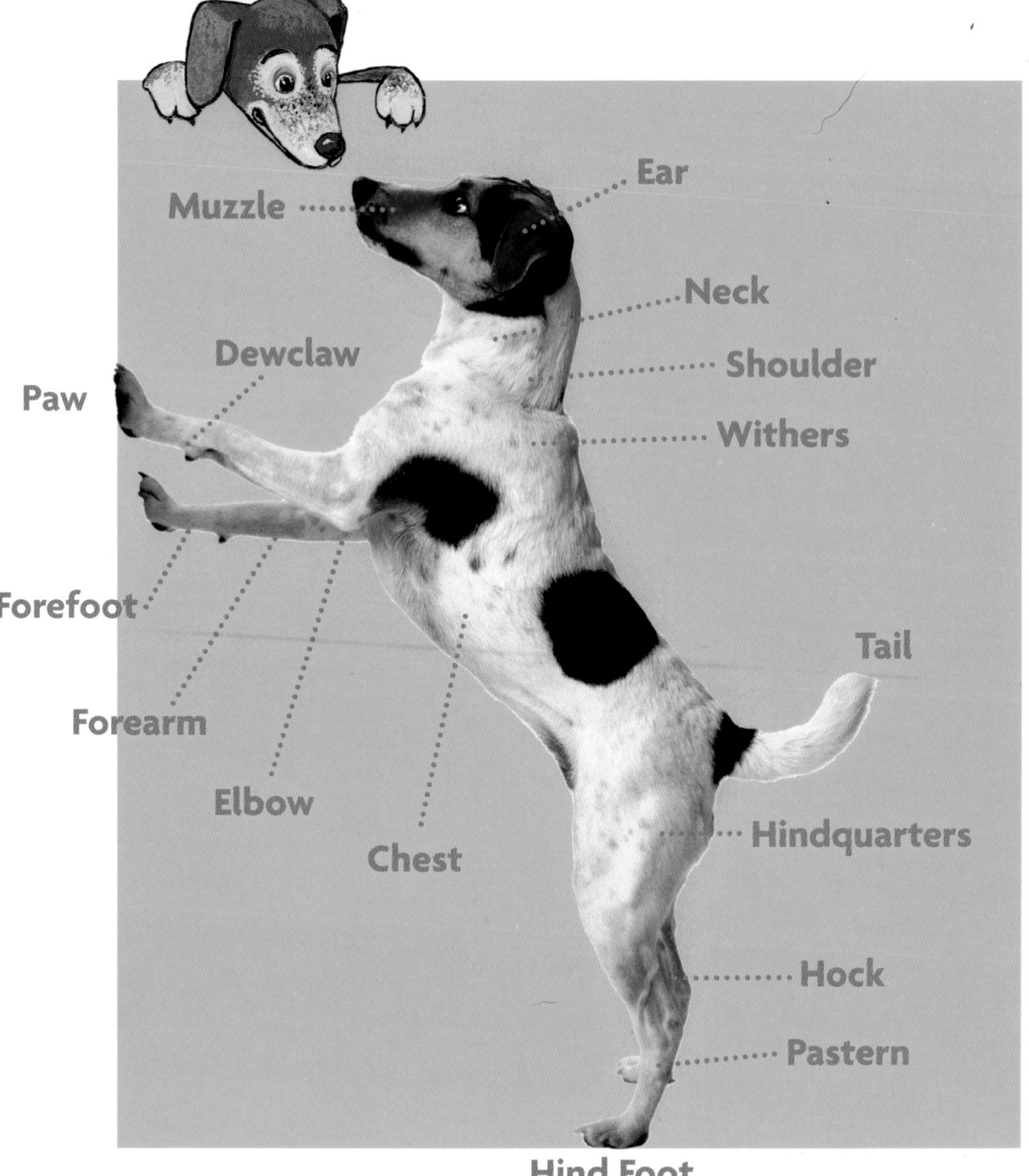
Ear
Muzzle
Neck
Dewclaw
Shoulder
Paw
Withers
Forefoot
Tail
Forearm
Elbow
Hindquarters
Chest
Hock
Pastern
Hind Foot

Name Game

Every dog deserves a good name! If you need a name for a four-legged friend—whether she's stuffed or real—see if any of these suit her to a tee.

For a devoted pup who won't leave your side, call her **Shadow, Sticks, Ghost**, or **Guide.**

Do you love to read? A character might do—
Charlotte, Dolittle, Madeline, or **Pooh.**

Cinnamon and **Ginger** are names to savor, but **Pepper** and **Jalapeño** have more flavor.

Try **Jelly Bean, Taffy**, or **Licorice**—
for really sweet dogs, check the candy dish!

Salty and **Sailor** have seaside flash if your dog loves the water and can't wait to splash.

Whatever name you pick will fit like a glove, as long as you choose it with kindness and love.

Fun Flavors

Pumpkin
Peaches
Cocoa
Honey
Cappuccino
Vanilla
Mocha
Sugar
Root Beer

Compute This

Google
Megabyte
Icon
Mac
Yahoo
Nano

Tailor-Made

Velvet
Lacey
Polka-dot
Paisley
Stitch
Patches
Buttons

Color Me!

Pinky
Sandy
Indigo
Violet
Red
Blackie

Red-Hot Ranks

Captain
Duke
Duchess
Princess
Sergeant
Chief

Playful Places

Orion
Timbuktu
Montana
Dakota
Madison
Paris

Just for Fun

Kibbles
Doodle
Iggy
Geezer
Digger
Sprocket

Food for Thought

Muffin
Marshmallow
Oreo
Cracker
Toast
Biscuit
Cookie
Brownie

Silly Sizes

Tiny
Peewee
Moose
Bigwig
Bitsy
Peanut

Sky-High

Star
Sunny
Rain
Stormy
Snowflake
Dawn
Lightning
Thunder
Rainbow
Midnight

Catchy Characters

Hermione
Ramona
Scout
Pippi
Harry
Toto
Wilbur
Fudge

Sounds Like . . .

Buzz
D-O-G (dee-oh-gee)
Bamm-Bamm
Boomer
Woof

Big Truth

To know dogs is to love them.

To learn more about dogs or programs in this book, visit these helpful Web sites:

akc.org
(American Kennel Club) has general information on dog breeds

caninecompanions.org
for information on Canine Companions for Independence, an organization that trains dogs to assist people with disabilities

deafdogs.org
for information about training or adopting a deaf dog

deltasociety.org
has information on how you and your dog can get involved with Pet Partners®

petfinder.com for information on adopting a homeless dog or locating a dog lost during a disaster

seeingeye.org for information about The Seeing Eye, Inc.

westminsterkennelclub.org for information on dog shows and more

American Girl cannot guarantee that sites listed will have all the information you need or that exact addresses won't change after this book is printed. Always share information you get online with your parents, and never give out personal information.

Send your comments to
Girls and their Dogs editor
American Girl
8400 Fairway Place
Middleton, WI 53562

(All comments and suggestions received by American Girl may be used without compensation or acknowledgment. Sorry—photos can't be returned.)

Here are some other American Girl books you might like:

❑ I read it.

❑ I read it.

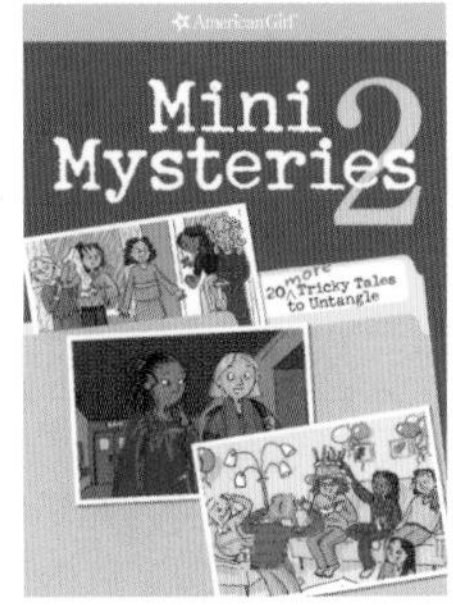

❑ I read it.

❑ I read it.

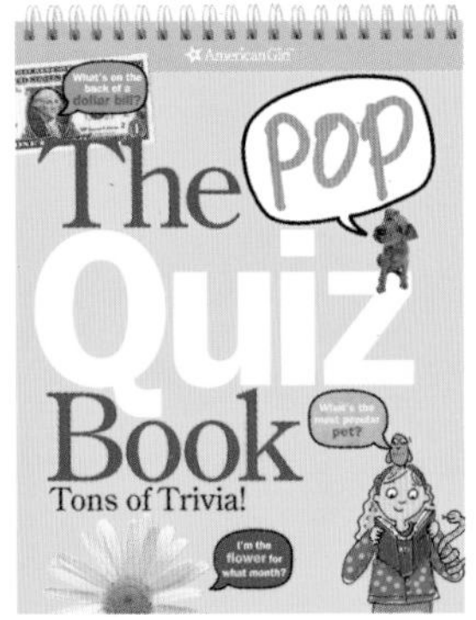

❑ I read it.

❑ I read it.